'Twas The First Night Of Christmas

For all ages

Pastor Lloyd E. Stinnett D. D.

WestBow Press books may be ordered through booksellers or by contacting:

WestBow Press
A Division of Thomas Nelson & Zondervan
1663 Liberty Drive
Bloomington, IN 47403
www.westbowpress.com
844-714-3454

Scripture taken from the King James Version of the Bible.

ISBN: 978-1-6642-4261-6 (sc)
ISBN: 978-1-6642-4262-3 (e)

Library of Congress Control Number: 2021916319

Print information available on the last page.

WestBow Press rev. date: 8/26/2021

WESTBOW
PRESS®
A DIVISION OF THOMAS NELSON
& ZONDERVAN

This book belongs to:

_____

Acknowledgements, with thanks and love to:

Jesus Christ for giving me the gift of writing.

Ollie Hayden
Rose Hayden
Arlon Benton Stinnett
Virginia L. Stinnett
Ronald Voland

Blondi

Design and Illustration

facebook: Blondi Design &illistration
Email:blondiart13@gmail.com

'Twas the first night of Christmas,
and we still can't get it right.
They say it's about Santa, but wasn't it Jesus,
Who was born that night?
For such a long time we forgot,
the truth of that day.
The true meaning of Christmas,
from which we have strayed.

Some just call it a holiday,
(Say next 4 lines nonchalantly.)
and don't recognize it at all.
Some like to decorate, buy gifts,
and others just have a ball.
But with all this confusion,
at this hectic time of year.
I will soon tell you my story,
and make it quite clear.

With all the gifts, decorations,
and the hustling we do.
As so many at this time,
are so lonely and blue.
All the Christmas songs about Jesus,
do we really hear what they say?
Or do we just listen to the music,
to past our time away?

Luke 2:1-14 K.J.V.: And it came to pass in those days, that there went out a decree from Caesar Augustus that all the world should be taxed. (And this taxing was first made when Cyrenius was governor of Syria.) And all went to be taxed, everyone into his own city. And Joseph also went up from Galilee, out of the city of Nazareth, into Judaea, unto the city of David, which is called Bethlehem. (He was of the house and lineage of David.) To be taxed with Mary his espoused wife, being great with Child. And so it was, that, while they were there, the days were accomplished that she should be delivered. And she brought forth her firstborn Son and wrapped Him in swaddling clothes and laid Him in a manger, because there was no room for them in the inn. And there were in the same country shepherds abiding in the field, keeping watch over their flock by night. And, lo, the angel of the Lord came upon them, and the glory of the Lord shone round about them: and they were sore afraid. And the angel said unto them, Fear not: for, behold, I bring you good tidings of great joy, which shall be to all people. For unto you is born this day in the city of David a Savior, which is Christ the Lord. And this shall be a sign unto you. Ye shall find the Babe wrapped in swaddling clothes, lying in a manger. And suddenly there was with the angel a multitude of the heavenly host praising God, and saying, Glory to God in the highest, and on earth peace, good will toward men.

Now let me tell you my version,
that you can listen to.
But different and not as good,
as **'Saint Luke Chapter Two'**.
Truly a beautiful story,
as it was to be for a sign.
About a beautiful little Baby,
from way back in time.

Please think hard of what,
I am about to say.
For without Him,
there would be no **'Christmas Day'.**
That little Baby was born in a stable
and not under a tree.

(Sing this line as from the song.)
Nor up on a housetop,
nor down a chimney.

The stable had a donkey
and a lamb that was near,
but I promise you folks,
there were no flying reindeer.

As the Shepherds were watching,
their sheep by night.
They heard the angels praising God,
but not an Elf was in sight.

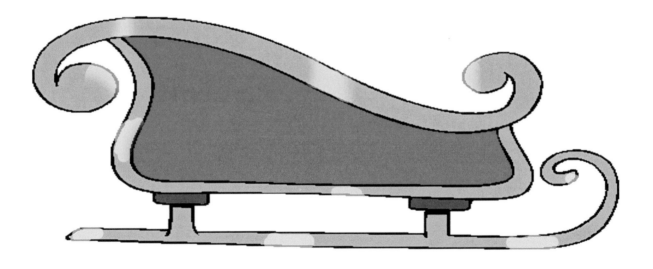

They went to the place,
where the **'Son of God'** lay,
But I'm telling you folks that they walked,
cause they had no magic sleigh.

The shepherds, wise men,
and people came from all around.
No place was there a Santa,
to be found.

Although I just love,
the manger scenes that we see.
It was a few years later,
for the three Wise Men were there to be.

While a man called Santa says, **"Ho, Ho, Ho"**,
(Say Ho, Ho, Ho loud.)
with great mirth.

But in honor of a
'Baby Jesus'
the angels sing,
for us to have
'Peace On Earth'.

The Wise Men brought three gifts,
as the scriptures did say.
But really, the first gift was given to us,
from God that day.

43 And whence *is* this to me, that the mother of my Lord should come to me?

44 For, lo, as soon as the voice of thy salutation sounded in mine ears, the babe leaped in my womb for joy.

45 And blessed *is* she that believed: for there shall be a performance of those things which were told her from the Lord.

46 And Ma'ry said, My soul doth magnify the Lord,

47 And my spirit hath rejoiced in God my Saviour.

★ 48 For he hath regarded the low estate of his handmaiden: for, behold, from henceforth all generations shall call me blessed.   *I Sam. 1:11; Mal. 3:12*

49 For he that is mighty hath done to me great things; and holy *is* his name.   *Ps. 71:19*

50 And his mercy *is* on them that fear him from generation to generation.   *Gen. 17:7; Ps. 103:17*

51 He hath shewed strength with his arm; he hath scattered the proud in the imagination of their hearts.

★ 52 He hath put down the mighty from *their* seats, and exalted them of low degree.   *I Sam. 2:5*

53 He hath filled the hungry with good things; and the rich he hath sent empty away.   *I Sam. 2:5*

54 He hath holpen his servant Is'-ra-el, in remembrance of *his* mercy;

55 As he spake to our fathers, to A'bra-ham, and to his seed for ever.

56 And Ma'ry abode with her about three months, and returned to her own house.

57 Now E-lis'a-beth's full time came that she should be delivered; and she brought forth a son.

58 And her neighbours and her cousins heard how the Lord had shewed great mercy upon her, and they rejoiced with her.

59 And it came to pass, that on the eighth day they came to circumcise the child; and they called him Zach-a-ri'as, after the name of his father.

60 And his mother answered and said, Not *so*; but he shall be called John.

61 And they said unto her, There is none of thy kindred that is called by this name.

62 And they made signs to his father, how he would have him called.

63 And he asked for a writing table, and wrote, saying, His name is John. And they marvelled all.

64 And his mouth was opened immediately, and his tongue *loosed*, and he spake, and praised God.

65 And fear came on all that dwelt round about them: and all these sayings were noised abroad throughout all the hill country of Ju-dæ'a.

66 And all they that heard *them* laid *them* up in their hearts, saying, What manner of child shall this be! And the hand of the Lord was with him.   *Gen. 39:2*

67 And his father Zach-a-ri'as was filled with the Ho'ly Ghost, and prophesied, saying,

68 Blessed *be* the Lord God of Is'-ra-el; for he hath visited and redeemed his people,

69 And hath raised up an horn of salvation for us in the house of his servant Da'vid;

70 As he spake by the mouth of his holy prophets, which have been since the world began: *Jer. 23:5; Acts 3:21*

71 That we should be saved from our enemies, and from the hand of all that hate us;

72 To perform the mercy *promised* to our fathers, and to remember his holy covenant;   *Lev. 26:42; Ezek. 16:60*

73 The oath which he sware to our father A'bra-ham,   *Gen. 12:3*

74 That he would grant unto us, that we being delivered out of the hand of our enemies might serve him without fear,   *Rom. 6:18; Heb. 9:14*

75 In holiness and righteousness before him, all the days of our life.

76 And thou, child, shalt be called the prophet of the Highest: for thou shalt go before the face of the Lord to prepare his ways;   *Isa. 40:3; Mal. 11:10*

77 To give knowledge of salvation unto his people by the remission of their sins,   *Or, for • Mark 1:4*

★ 78 Through the tender mercy of our God; whereby the dayspring from on high hath visited us,

79 To give light to them that sit in darkness and in the shadow of death, to guide our feet into the way of peace.   *Isa. 9:2; Acts 26:18*

80 And the child grew, and waxed strong in spirit, and was in the deserts till the day of his shewing unto Is'ra-el.   *Mal. 3:1*

2 And it came to pass in those days, that there went out a decree from Cæ'sar Au-gus'tus, that all the world should be taxed.   *Or, enrolled*

2 (*And* this taxing was first made when Cy-re'ni-us was governor of Syr'i-a.)   *Acts 5:37*

3 And all went to be taxed, every one into his own city.

4 And Jo'seph also went up from Gal'i-lee, out of the city of Naz'a-reth, into Ju-dæ'a, unto the city of Da'vid, which is called Beth'le-hem; (because he was of the house and lineage of Da'vid:)   *I Sam. 16:1; Matt. 1:16*

5 To be taxed with Ma'ry his espoused wife, being great with child.

6 And so it was, that, while they were there, the days were accomplished that she should be delivered.

7 And she brought forth her firstborn son, and wrapped him in swaddling clothes, and laid him in a manger; because there was no room for them in the inn.   *Matt. 1:25*

8 And there were in the same country shepherds abiding in the field, keeping watch over their flock by night.   *Or, the night watches*

9 And, lo, the angel of the Lord came upon them, and the glory of the Lord shone round about them: and they were sore afraid.   *Luke 1:12*

★ 10 And the angel said unto them, Fear not: for, behold, I bring you good tidings of great joy, which shall be to all people.   *Gen. 12:3; Mark 1:15*

11 For unto you is born this day in the city of Da'vid a Saviour, which is Christ the Lord.   *Isa. 9:6; Luke 1:43*

12 And this *shall be* a sign unto you; Ye shall find the babe wrapped in swaddling clothes, lying in a manger.

13 And suddenly there was with the angel a multitude of the heavenly host praising God, and saying,

14 Glory to God in the highest, and on earth peace, good will toward men.   *Isa. 57:19; John 3:16; Eph. 1:6*

15 And it came to pass, as the angels were gone away from them into heaven, the shepherds said one to another, Let us now go even unto

The gift of **'Salvation'** is why,
all this was done.
Of the birth, the suffering, and the death,
of **'God's Only Son'.**
Just read the word in scriptures,
that God put down in print.

Just open your heart to it.
Do not be like that
'Mean Old Ebenezer Scrooge',
who was a ***Skinflint*.**

Mark 8:36 N.K.J.V.: For what will it profit a man if he gains the whole world, and loses his own soul?

*A person who would gain or extort money by any means also known as a miser.

So, don't be so cold,
(Say **'COLD'** as if it is freezing.)
like a snowman called Frosty.

John 3:16 King James Version: For God so loved the world that He gave His only begotten Son, that whoever believes in Him should not perish but have everlasting life.

So, in denying this gift,
you will find it to be most costly.
So, the true **'Reason For This Season'**,
it's really quite clear.
It should be something we hold close to our hearts,
so precious and dear.

I know that my version is quite different,
than others have wrote.
But we've come so far from the scriptures,
and that is no joke.

So this time of year,
take time to think, but don't wait.
Please take **'God's Gift Of 'Salvation',**
before it's too late.

I have written some other children's books. One is out now called: **'Ruffles The Dragon.'** Watch out for episode II called: **'Ruffles' Scuffle.'** Also, I have the first book of six episodes out called: **'A Flea, A Fly, And A Mouse.'** Also, coming out soon is a Christian children's book called: **'The Witness.'**

And for the adults I have a few books out now. Four Christian books called: **'Many Things Most Christians Do Not Know,' 'A Must Read For Everyone,' 'The Mystery Book,'** and **'Live Life, Laughter, And Love.'** I also wrote a poetry book called: **'Laughter, Inspiration, Spiritual, And Tears.'** Also coming out maybe this year, will be a book called: **'It's So Funny.'**

These books can be bought at Amazon, Barnes and Noble, and 25,000-30,000 retailers around the world.

**'With Love In Christ,
And Stay Safe.'**
Pastor Lloyd E. Stinnett D. D.

By the way, are you going to church? I sure hope so. If not, there are plenty of fun things to do there and much to learn. And maybe if your mom and dad are not going, you can get them to go too.

Printed in the United States
by Baker & Taylor Publisher Services